14 99

Portsmouth – Kittery Naval Shipyard

IN OLD PHOTOGRAPHS

Portsmouth – Kittery Naval Shipyard

IN OLD PHOTOGRAPHS

Collected by
ROBERT H. WHITTAKER

Alan Sutton Publishing Limited
Phoenix Mill · Far Thrupp
Stroud · Gloucestershire

First published 1993

Library of Congress Cataloging in Publication
Data applied for

Typeset in 9/10 Sabon.
Typesetting and origination by
Alan Sutton Publishing Limited.
Printed in Great Britain by
Redwood Books, Trowbridge, Wiltshire.

Motto insignia of the Portsmouth Naval Shipyard. (PNSM)

Contents

Dedicated to My Wife Robin

Introduction

Naval ship construction in America had its beginning in 1690 on the shores of the Piscataqua River, which serves as a natural boundary between Maine and New Hampshire. Though only a few Royal Navy ships were constructed here, colonial building ways were soon controlled by American sympathizers during the revolution, resulting in the construction of at least three US warships. In 1799 chief naval constructor Humphries recommended to the Secretary of the Navy that Portsmouth Harbor be the site of a government owned and operated shipyard, the swift waters, upriver islands, and ready source of materials and skilled labor being all the reason he would need to convince Congress to allocate $5,500 for the purchase of Fernalds Island in Portsmouth Harbor on 12 June 1800.

Through all major national conflicts the Portsmouth Naval Shipyard (PNS) was called upon to design and construct warships – from the War of 1812 to the Vietnam War. 'Sails to Atoms' is the shipyard's motto. From the ship of the line *Washington*, launched in 1815, to the fast attack nuclear submarine USS *Sand Lance*, launched in 1969, the PNS distinguished itself as a leader in naval design and construction.

In 1914 the PNS was assigned the task of designing and building the first government-built submarine which resulted in the launching of the L-8 in 1917. This became the only US sub to see action during the First World War. From 1917 to 1969, 137 submarines were built at PNS. Those subs constructed for the Second World War were among the finest, according to veterans of the war who served on them with great anticipation and relief, for these were the first subs in the fleet to be equipped with air conditioning.

Post Second World War was a transitional period for the submarine until 1953, when the USS *Albacore* was launched. The diesel electric experimental sub, designed at PNS, marked the beginning of a new era for sub technology. The *Albacore*'s revolutionary tear-drop hull design and propulsion system helped to launch the modern submarine fleet into the twenty-first century. During the 1960s PNS built several nuclear subs in the fast attack and ballistic missile classes.

In the preparation of this introduction and the collection of photographs which follow, I could not have done without the unselfish help given so willingly by Jim Dolph, curator of the Portsmouth Naval Shipyard Museum and Visitor's Center. His wealth of knowledge pertaining to the shipyard's history was of great assistance in putting captions to the photos. Also, acknowledgement and appreciation go to the Portsmouth Naval Shipyard for allowing me access to its museum's photographic archives, which, along with volumes of documents, literature, and artefacts, makes the museum and the fifty historic sites on the shipyard a bona fide national treasure. An entire fifty-acre section of the shipyard has been preserved in such a way as to give one a feel for how a nineteenth-century shipyard might have looked long ago.

From 1974 to present day PNS has continued its leadership role in areas of overhauling and repairing submarines. In this world of uncertainties as to where the United States Navy may next be called to defend its country, there is one thing which is certain, that the tremendous human resource found at the Portsmouth Naval Shipyard will be there to meet whatever challenges the future may hold, as it has done so remarkably for nearly two hundred years of service to America.

Because I consider the shipyard operation vital and the importance of its history worth preserving for all Americans, I dedicate proceeds that I will realize through the sale of this book to the Portsmouth Naval Shipyard Museum.

Robert H. Whittaker

(Credit legend: NHC = Naval Historical Center; PNSM = Portsmouth Naval Shipyard Museum; NHF = Naval Historical Foundation; LOC = Library of Congress; USN = US Navy.)

Portsmouth Naval Shipyard, 1800–1900

Welcome to the Portsmouth Naval Shipyard, Gate #1, *c.* 1970. (USN)

The monument to the continental Sloop of War *Ranger*. This vessel was the first US Naval warship to fly the Stars and Stripes, a flag made from dress material belonging to Portsmouth women. The monument was erected in 1905. (NHC)

IOHN PAUL IONES,
Commander of a Squadron in the Service of
THE THIRTEEN UNITED STATES OF NORTH AMERICA, 1779.

Portrait of Captain John Paul Jones, *c.* 1779. He was born in Scotland and christened John Paul; the 'Jones' was added later in America to obscure his real identity if captured. As the father of the US Navy, he is honored by having his remains entombed in the chapel at the United States Naval Academy, Annapolis, Maryland. (LOC)

Captain John Paul Jones on deck of *Serapis*, giving a farewell salute to his ship, the *Bon Homme Richard*. Jones helped to establish Portsmouth as an early naval shipbuilding port. (PNSM)

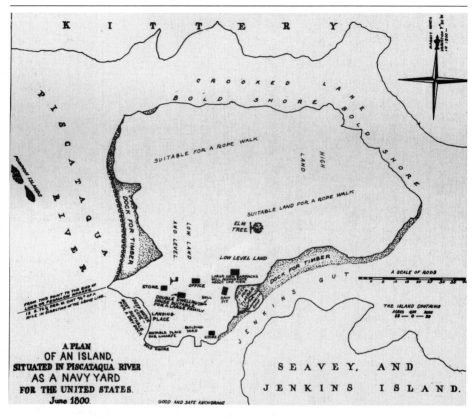

A PLAN
OF AN ISLAND,
SITUATED IN PISCATAQUA RIVER
AS A NAVY YARD
FOR THE UNITED STATES.
June 1800.

Fernald's or 'Lay Claim' Island as it appeared when purchased from William Dennett by the Navy on 12 June 1800 for $5,500. Portsmouth Naval Shipyard was established on this island and is considered to be the oldest publicly held navy yard in the US under continuous operation. (PNSM)

Commodore Isaac Hull, first commander of Portsmouth Naval Shipyard from 1813 to 1815 and former commander of the Boston Navy Yard and famed *Old Ironsides*. (PNSM)

Quarters 'A', the home of the commanding officer at PNS. Built by local joiner John Locke during the War of 1812 for the first yard commander, Isaac Hull, this is the oldest building on the shipyard. It is among the 50 yard buildings which are listed on the National Register of Historic Places. (PNSM)

The spiral staircase in Quarters 'A'. 'Its delicate balusters are toed into dado treds, supported by handcrafted rails that flow from their easements, newel posts and gooseneck ramps.' (PNS Quarters 'A' booklet) (PNSM)

USS *Cumberland* at PNS in 1859. (PNSM)

Marine Barracks was built by the Marines themselves in 1828 at north end of the shipyard, in an area known for its snakes and justly named Snakehill. The parade grounds were leveled by prisoners. Marines first arrived at the yard in 1806. (PNSM)

Building 5, built in 1820s, stood where present day building ways shed is located. (PNSM)

Muster Room, Building 13, upon completion in 1859. It once served as the shipyard's headquarters. 'The clock in the tower is reputed to be the first clock in the US Navy to strike ship's bells rather than hours. H.H. Ham, a shipyard worker, received the patent rights to the striking mechanism on 6 May 1879. This mechanism has since been repaired but not altered.' (*A History of Portsmouth Naval Shipyard*) (PNSM)

The clockworks in Building 13. Counterweights still have to be wound weekly. (USN)

Louisiana live oak taken from Pensicola, Florida, for use in the USS *Constitution* rebuild of the 1920s. Many of these timbers are still 'soaking' in a man-made fresh water pond on yard once used to supply water for shipyard steam engines. (USN)

USS *Constitution*. On 7 June 1855 the 2,200 ton frigate arrived at PNS for conversion to a training tallship for naval cadets. She is shown here as a receiving ship and sometime museum, and was often used as function facilities by, for example, the masons who line the railing. She served in this capacity from 1882–97, when she was towed to Boston in celebration of the 100th anniversary of her launching. (PNSM)

Interior view of the enclosed main deck of USS *Constitution* at PNS, 1880s–90s. (PNSM)

The USS *Constitution* secured alongside the quay on the main channel of the Piscataqua River. Behind the stone masthouse are two shiphouses built around 1890. (PNSM)

Yeomen with oars posing in front of the USS *Constitution*, *c.* 1890. (PNSM)

The shipyard riverfront quay with PNS-built USS *Portsmouth* secured ahead of USS *Constitution* in front of Building 5, *c.* 1880s.

USS *Portsmouth* was launched at the yard on 10 November 1844 as a new class sloop of war at 1,022 tons and 153 ft in length. Her first captain was Commander John B. Montgomery, who helped to open trade with Japan and had his ship stand watch over San Francisco while US troops took California from Mexico in 1846. She later served alongside Royal Navy warships on patrol on the west coast of Africa in an attempt to stem the flow of slaves from the region. She was retired from the navy on 17 April 1915. (PNSM)

USS *Minnesota* in 1865, shown in the floating dry dock which was built at the yard in 1852. Note the smoke stack for steam boiler. (PNSM)

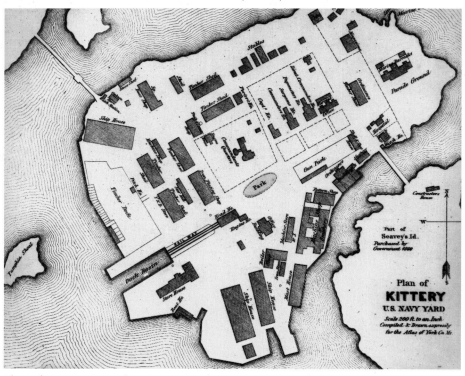

Plan of PNS in 1868 during post-Civil War expansion of the yard after surviving the talks of closure. (PNSM)

Standing in front of the Franklin House is the saluting battery built in 1876, seen here in the late nineteenth century. When ships arrived at PNS guns would fire the traditional salute. (PNSM)

The patented Stevenson's wood timber bending machine, invented by one Augusta Stevenson, who was employed as a yard shipwright for several years. (PNSM)

Admiral David Glasgow Farragut, US Navy, became the first admiral of the navy and died in Quarters 'A' on 14 August 1870 at the age of 70. During the famed Battle of Mobile Bay on 5 August 1864 he cried out, 'Damn the torpedos, full speed ahead!' in defiance of mines set in his ship's path by the Confederate navy as he entered the bay. (PNSM)

The plaque in honor of Admiral Farragut was dedicated on 26 August 1908. The inscription was written by Admiral George Dewey and is located on the iron fence in front of Quarters 'A'. (PNSM)

The USS *Tallaposa* (far right), which brought Admiral Farragut to PNS on 4 July 1870. The ship also escorted the relief fleet that brought the survivors of the Lady Bay Franklin Greely Arctic Expedition to PNS in August 1884. Other ships at the yard are likely the relief fleet. (PNSM)

Adolphus Greely sporting his Arctic coat on arrival at PNS. (PNSM)

The relief fleet which brought the Greely Arctic Expedition to PNS. The westerly winds were stiff that day as the fleet waited at anchor off Kittery Point. Left to right: *Tallaposa*, *Alliance*, *Thetis* and *Bear*. (PNSM)

This ship is possibly the *Thetis* at PNS in 1884, serving as one of relief fleet vessels for the Greely Arctic Expedition. (PNSM)

Building 14, built as the headhouse in the 1880s to operate a marine railway. (PNSM)

The Howitzer shed was built in the shipyard's ordnance park in 1865.

The USS *Agamenticus*, a double turretted monitor mounted with four guns, was constructed of wood and sheathed with iron plating. Built at PNS in 1864, the boat was later renamed the *Terror*. (PNSM)

Naval cadets aboard the USS *Constellation*, *c*. 1861. (NHC)

The first bridge built between Kittery and the shipyard in 1825, shown here in 1876. (NHF)

Major John H. Hipbee, USMC, was commanding officer of the shipyard's Marine Barracks from 1888 to 1895. (NHC)

Department of Yards and Docks personnel, 1878. Many of these people are ancestors of present day shipyard workers. (PSNM)

After the Spanish American War a marine camp was established in the shipyard, named Camp Heywood in honor of the Commandant of the Marine Corps. The camp became the home of Col. Huntington's Battalion until the unit was disbanded. (PNSM)

Group of Marine Officers, First Battalion Marines, PNS, 1898. Left to right: 1st Lieut. Lewis C. Lucas, 1st Lieut. Clarence L.A. Ingate, 2nd Lieut. Melville J. Shaw, 2nd Lieut. Newt H. Hall, 2nd Lieut. Don A. Thaxter. (NHC)

Photo of the famous horse 'Old Tom' at PNS taken several years after the Spanish American War. Col. Huntington, USMC, led the First Battalion of marines to Cuba and rode 'Old Tom' into battle. 'Old Tom' is buried at the shipyard. (PNSM)

Building 31, Magazine House, built in the 1840s. (PSNM)

Spanish prisoners of war at PSNY in 1898. (PSNM)

S.J. Skaw fired the first shot on board USS *Olympia* at the Battle of Manila, 1898. (PNSM)

There were 1,600 Spanish prisoners of war at PNS after the Spanish American War in 1898. (PNSM)

Graves of Spanish Prisoners · Portsmouth Navy Yard

A postcard view showing the graves of Spanish prisoners at PNS at the turn of the century. These Spanish prisoners died while imprisoned at the shipyard during the Spanish American War of 1898. (PNSM)

Monument marking the imprisonment of Spanish prisoners of war at PSN. (PNSM)

Blue Jackets (Marine Corps), Market Square, Portsmouth, New Hampshire, 1898. (NHC)

USS *Maine* at anchor off Portsmouth Harbor during the summer of 1897. (PNSM)

USS *Wisconsin*, PNS, in for repairs in 1909. (PNSM)

The anchor of the USS *Tallaposa* serving as a memorial to Admiral David D. Porter, the famed Civil War hero who served at PNS as Ordnance Officer prior to the war. *Tallaposa* was a Civil War steamship used in the east coast blockade of Confederate states. (PNSM)

Building 89 was built as a hospital in 1891, later serving as a Bachelors Officers' Quarters. The building is now used for academic apprentice programs. (USN)

Portsmouth Naval Shipyard, 1900–1920

The turn of the century brought expanded facilities at PSN. This photograph shows the west cofferdam for the new dry dock, 8 March 1900. (PNSM)

PNS on 22 August 1901, showing water standpipe in the foreground near ponds used for steam engines on the yard. In the left background, looking across the Piscataqua River, is the Wentworth-by-the-Sea grand summer resort built in 1873. (PNSM)

Cannons on the Mall at PNS, c. 1902. (USN)

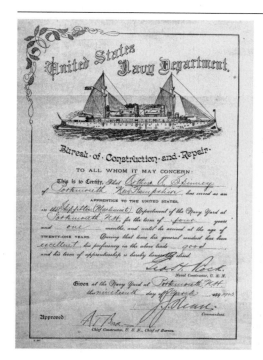

Graduation Certificate closing the apprenticeship of Arthur Spinney at PNS awarded to him on 19 March 1902. (PNSM)

U.S. NAVY YARD,

Portsmouth, N. H. *Aug. 11* 190*4*

Pass *J. E. Patch*

by boat to and from landing No. *2*.

Luther E. Gregory

CIVIL ENGINEER, U. S. N,

Head of Department

Captain of the Yard.

A navy yard worker's pass by boat to and from landing #2. The pass was for J.E. Patch. (PNSM)

Henderson's Point, Seavy Island, PNS, 1904. (PNSM)

Wooden floating dry dock. It was towed from PNS in 1907. (PNSM)

In 1905 two landmark events occurred at PNS which made Portsmouth famous in the eyes of the world: the largest explosion in the history of mankind (to date) on 22 July and the Treaty of Portsmouth signed in Building 86 on 5 September. Shown here is the excavation work at Henderson's Point prior to the explosion. (PNSM)

Henderson's Point cofferdam, showing the crew carrying an 80-ft drill to the drill site, 1905. (PNSM)

Henderson's Point, showing another view of the cofferdam, 1905. The land fill in the foreground is excavation material. (PNSM)

Delegations from Russia and Japan in Building 86 during final negotiations that led to the signing of the Treaty of Portsmouth which ended the Russo-Japanese War of 1905. (PNSM)

IN THIS BUILDING,
AT THE INVITATION OF
THEODORE ROOSEVELT,
PRESIDENT OF THE UNITED STATES,
WAS HELD THE
PEACE CONFERENCE
BETWEEN THE
ENVOYS OF RUSSIA AND JAPAN,
AND
SEPTEMBER 5, 1905, AT 3.47 P.M.,
WAS SIGNED
THE TREATY OF PORTSMOUTH,
WHICH ENDED THE WAR BETWEEN THE TWO EMPIRES.

Commemoration plaque, located on the front of the building, honoring the Treaty of Portsmouth signing. (PNSM)

Building 86, where the Treaty of Portsmouth was signed at 3:47 p.m. on 5 September 1905. (PNSM)

Henderson's Point, viewed from Pierce Island, prior to explosion. A blast on 22 July 1905 removed the remaining ledge of the point. (PNSM)

Moment of blast during the world's largest explosion to date on 22 July 1905 at Henderson's Point. A charge of 50 tons of dynamite was used in the explosion. (PNSM)

Blast sight of Henderson's Point shortly after the explosion. (PNSM)

PNS Bridge from Kittery, showing the Franklin Building which was constructed in 1838 and was considered one of the largest wooden shiphouses in the US at 240 ft long, 131 ft wide, and 72 ft to the ridge pole. Its roof was covered with 130 tons of slate. (PNSM)

Dry dock construction, *c.* 1900. (PNSM)

Dry Dock #2 after completion, showing a collier, the first ship to enter the dock. Also shown are the shears at the coaling station on the left and the old steam crane on the right side of the dock. (NHC)

The *Southery* in the back channel at PNS served as a prison ship between 1903 and 1920. She also served as a pig processing plant, with prisoners providing the labor. (PNSM)

Chief Boatswain William Lowell Hill was commanding officer of the *Southery*. (PNSM)

Prisoners mustering up ratlines aboard the *Southery*. (PNSM)

Naval prisoners on the dock between prison ship *Southery* on the left and the USS *Topeka* on the right, *c.* 1915. (LOC)

NAVAL PRISON PORTSMOUTH N.H.   (front)

The Naval Prison at PNS, on the eastern end of Seavey's Island, was begun in 1905 and received its first prisoners in 1908. Bedding is being aired in the foreground. (PNSM)

Prisoners were in charge of many duties, including mess hall detail. (PNSM)

Laundry room in the Naval Prison. (PNSM)

The marine guard force are sporting winter gear in front of the prison. (PNSM)

Prisoners returning from work in various shops on the navy yard. (PNSM)

Prisoners and their guard in front of the prison. (PNSM)

Interior view of a single cell located in the centre of the prison. (PNSM)

Dry Dock Basin #1 was constructed in 1852 to receive the new floating dry dock built at the shipyard. During the Second World War it was converted to a permanent dry dock. (PNSM)

View of PNS in the early 1900s, showing a warship being manoeuvered in the back channel past the Franklin Shiphouse. (PNSM)

A ship being manoeuvered into the coaling dock at PNS, *c.* 1915. (PNSM)

The Billiard Hall in the men's reading room, 8 March 1915. (PNSM)

Bowling alleys in the men's reading room, 8 March 1915. (PNSM)

Naval Reserve camp during the First World War at PNS. (PNSM)

Panoramic view of PNS, looking from Portsmouth, with the cross-river ferry in the foreground, *c.* 1920. (NHC)

Exterior view of the submarine model shed at PNS on 29 September 1917. (NHC)

The police force at PNS in 1918. (NHC)

Female yeomen practising for the Boston Regatta in 1918 on the Piscataqua River. (NHC)

Industrial Office military and civilian personnel at PNS on 28 January 1919. (NHC)

Women shipyard workers manufacturing bread pans in October 1918. (NHC)

Women shipyard workers manufacturing cargo nets in October 1918. (NHC)

Construction progress of the new submarine ways at the yard on 29 October 1917. (NHC)

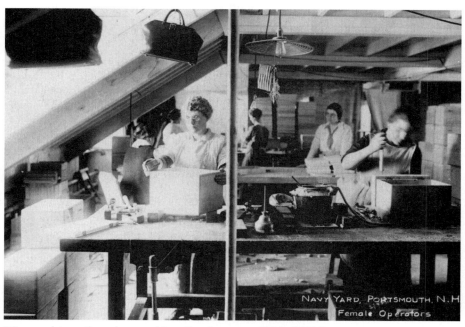

Women shipyard workers making ditty boxes, c. 1920. (NHC)

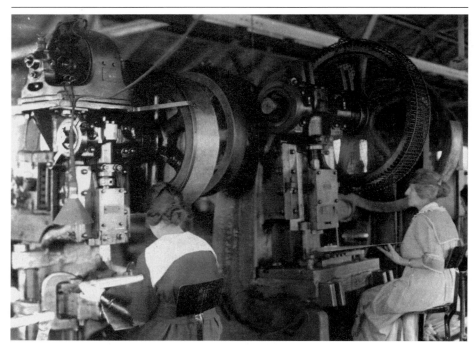

Women shipyard workers operating the bending press, *c.* 1918. (NHC)

US ships at PNS, showing the *Castine*, *Topeka*, *Eagle*, and the tug *Nazinscott*. This is a postcard photo from Morman Loring's collection dated 1907. (PNSM)

The YMCA building shown in front of the prison in March 1919. (NHC)

Recruits at PNS training camp in August 1917. (NHC)

Market Square, Portsmouth, New Hampshire, decorated in celebration of Armistice Day, 11 November 1918. (PNSM)

Parade leaving PNS during Armistice Day celebrations. (PNSM)

SECTION THREE

Beginning of the New Submarine Era

The *Holland* was commissioned into the navy on 12 October 1900, the date generally accepted as the beginning of the US submarine service. She was built at Crescent Shipyard in Elizabeth, NJ, by J.P. Holland and later used as a cadet training sub before being sold for scrap on 18 June 1913.

J.P. Holland, inventor of the first submarines in the modern era, photographed during inspection of a sub in 1895. (PNSM)

Simon Lake, submarine developer, seen here in 1895. (PNSM)

Bridge to the navy yard, with a view of Kittery in the background. (PNSM)

Navy yard fire department workers experimenting with seawater to make cement, *c.* 1920. (PNSM)

The L-8 at her launching on 23 April 1917. The first submarine built at a US Naval shipyard, as well as the only US sub to see action in the First World War, she is seen here coming down the ways of the Franklin Shiphouse. After serving patrols in both the Pacific and the Atlantic Oceans, the L-8 was decommissioned on 15 November 1922, then sold for scrap on 21 December 1925. (PNSM)

The L-8 (SS-48) after launching. The submarine was 165 ft long by 14 ft 9 inches wide and had four 18 inch torpedo tubes and a 1,200 bhp diesel engine for surface runs and recharging the batteries which powered an 800 hp electric motor for submerged runs. Her design depth was 200 ft. (PNS)

The L-8 on launching day, with a tug moving it in to dock. (PNSM)

The R-2, undergoing repairs at PNS, was built at Fore River Shipbuilding Co., Quincy, MA, in January 1918. (USN)

Gym workout at PNS, *c.* 1920. (PNS)

During the winter of 1918 a long deep cold spell was followed by a sudden January thaw, causing Great Bay ice to clog the lower river trapping the cross-river ferry. (PNSM)

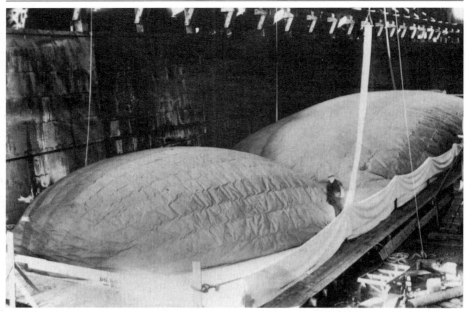

A non-rigid dirigible, built by a German contracting firm, being inflated at PNS on 22 December 1915. (NHC)

The dirigible following inflation. (NHC)

Female yeomen at PNS in May 1919. (PNSM)

Commandant's barge and crew at the back channel landing stage, PNS, September 1922. (PNSM)

The launching of the first and only O-1 built at PNS on 9 July 1918. She was not commissioned until after the Armistice, and saw service along the east coast until 28 December 1930, when she was converted to an experimental sub. She was decommissioned on 11 June 1931 and sold for scrap.

The S-3 on a test run out of Portsmouth Harbor. She was commissioned on 30 January 1919 and had a crew of four officers and thirty enlisted sailors. She had a design depth of 200 ft and carried twelve torpedoes, with a surface speed of 12 kn and a submerged speed of 11 kn. (PNSM)

The USS Barracuda after launching at PNS. Commissioned on 1 October 1924, she saw service during the Second World War and conducted six war patrols. She was decommissioned on 3 March 1945. (PNSM)

A ship and three submarines in PNS dry dock #2, c. 1920. The subs were captured German U-boats from the First World War. (PNSM)

PNS fire department team of horses in June 1922. (PNSM)

Yard workers testing the use of concrete in seawater on 17 June 1925. (PNSM)

Draftsmen at PNS in 1931. (PNSM)

The inspection party examining specimens of concrete tested in seawater on 5 April 1926.

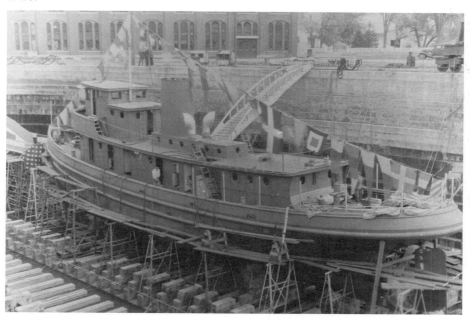

The Coast Guard cutter *Hudson* in PNS dry dock, *c.* 1930. (PNSM)

The USS *Narwhal* (V-5), built at PNS and commissioned on 15 May 1930 as a fleet submarine, came with a cost of $5,300,000. The *Narwhal* was one of five subs which docked in Pearl Harbor on 7 December 1941 and took part in the first victory for US Forces in the Pacific War at the Battle of Midway from 3–6 June 1941. She also played a major part during the evacuation of the Philippines. During the war the *Narwhal* conducted fourteen war patrols and sank approximately 20,000 tons of enemy shipping. She was retired on 23 April 1945 and sold for scrap. (PNSM)

The USS *Plunger* (SS-179), launched at PNS and commissioned on 19 November 1936, was cruising off Diamond Head when Japanese planes bombed Pearl Harbor. During the war she received fourteen battle stars followed by years as a Navy Reserve training sub until she was decommissioned on 5 July 1956. (PNSM)

A general view from the coaling plant, looking north-west and showing the extension of shipbuilding ways as seen on 10 July 1939. (PNSM)

The Franklin Shiphouse fire at 0500 hours, 10 March 1936. (PNSM)

By 0850 hours only ashes and twisted metal remained from the great fire which destroyed the Franklin Shiphouse. (PNSM)

Second World War Submarines and Their Builders

Out of control, the *Squalus* rears from the bottom.' (James A. Jones, *Boston Post*) This picture was taken on 13 July 1939 during a failed attempt to refloat the sub, which sank 5 miles south of the Isles of Shoals in 240 ft of water on her nineteenth test dive. Though thirty-three men were saved, twenty-six lost their lives. (PNSM)

USS *Squalus* (SS-192) salvage squadron at berth #5, PNS, on 9 July 1939. The USS *Sagamore* is alongside lighter barge #625, while USS *Wandank* pontoon #5 and #10 are along her outboard rail. Compare the size of chain laid out on dock to the car. (USN)

Squalus was towed to berth #6 for pumping out after a successful raising. (USN)

The *Squalus* in dry dock where she underwent a complete refit and was recommissioned as the *Sailfish* a year later. (USN)

USS *Sculpin* (SS-191) found the sunken sub's phone buoy shortly after the *Squalus* went down. Communications between the subs were made before the line broke. *Sailfish* went on to sink a Japanese ship carrying twenty crewmen from the *Sculpin* who had survived their sub's sinking; all but one was lost. (PNSM)

The *Squalus'* sail was saved after the war while the rest of her was scrapped. The sail rests in the PNS Mall along with *Tallaposa*'s anchor. (USN)

THIS·MEMORIAL·IS·DEDICATED·TO
ALL·MEN·OF·THE·U.S.SUBMARINE·FORCE
U.S.S.SQUALUS
BUILT·AT·U.S.NAVY·YARD,PORTSMOUTH,N.H.
COMMISSIONED·1·MARCH·1939·SUNK·OFF·ISLES·OF
SHOALS·23·MAY·1939·RAISED·FROM·40·FATHOMS
AND·REBUILT·BY·THE·NAVY·YARD.
·RECOMMISSIONED·AS·THE·
U.S.S.SAILFISH
SHE·ESTABLISHED·A·BRILLIANT·RECORD·IN·WORLD
WAR·II·WHICH·WAS·CLIMAXED·BY·THE·SINKING·OF
THE·LARGE·JAPANESE·AIRCRAFT·CARRIER·CHUYO
ON·4·DECEMBER·1943,
FOR·THIS·SHE·WAS·AWARDED·THE
PRESIDENTIAL·UNIT·CITATION.

The *Squalus* memorial plaque. (PNSM)

Barracks and mess of the submarine crew under construction on 2 October 1940, looking south with the prison in the background. (PNSM)

Marine tablet at the navy yard entrance in Maine. (PNSM)

War Bond sales drive at PNS, WHAB broadcast, 6 October 1942. Left to right: William Laird, shop 72; H.L. Robbins, shop 17; Carl T. Smart, public works; A.C. Phillips, Labor Board. (NHC)

Presidential yacht *Patomac* off quay at PNS. (PNSM)

President Franklin D. Roosevelt arriving at PNS for inspection at 0920 hours on 10 August 1940. Accompanying the president were NH Governor Murphy, Secretary of the Navy Knox, and RAdm. Wainwright. (PNSM)

The president with his son while inspecting the PNS on 10 August 1940. (PNSM)

French submarine *Surcouf* off PNS. The sub was a behemoth compared to contemporary US subs at more than 4,000 tons and 361 ft in length. She was equipped with two 8 inch guns and a sea plane hangar. She spent several months at the yard for repairs during the fall of 1941. (PNS)

Surcouf in PNS dry dock. (PNSM)

Wartime rally during the Second World War at PNS on 15 December 1941. (NHC)

Shop 38, outside machine and pipe shop supervisory force, 15 July 1940. Top row, left to right: Kimball, Fowles, Leibmen, Tibbits, Draper, Hennessy, Craig, Pierce. Middle row: Atwell, Huntress, Spinney, Buckley, Congulin, Gould, Stevens, Morang. Bottom row: Chick, Bridges, Bedell, Chandler (master mechanic), Frank, Patrick, Paul. (PNSM)

Woman shipyard worker operating a drill press during the Second World War. (PNSM)

Railroad car loaded with cannonballs being sent out for scrap iron salvage at PNS during the Second World War. (PNSM)

F.S.WHITE
MASTER RIGGER & LABORER

W.J.HARGEN-MASTER SMITH SHOP

J.E.NICHOLSON-MASTER PATTERNMAKER

H.L.ROBBINS
MASTER SHEETMETA

W.M.CHICK-MASTER
PIPE COPPER & PLUMBING

T.J.GAMESTER-MASTER
SHIPFITTER & BOILERMAKER

C.B.STEPHENSON
MASTER-TRANSPO

M.A.BARRETT-MASTER MACHINIST
ELECTRICAL

R.E.GOLDSMITH-MASTER MACHINIST
INSIDE

J.A.PETHIC-MASTER ELECTRICIAN

E.R.PRUETT-MASTER
JOINER & SHIPWRIGHT

R.G.BEDELL-MASTER
MACHINIST-OUTSIDE

R.N.SPINNEY
MASTER TOOLMAKER

W.J.MONAGLE
MASTER MOLDER

J.A.GREGOIRE
MASTER PAINTER

C.R.HARDING
MASTER POWER PLANT

H.W.HODGDON-MAS
BUILDING TRADES

Proud workers of PNS during the Second World War.

USS *Seawolf* (SS-197), commissioned at PNS on 1 December 1939, seen here on 5 August 1940. While serving in the Pacific during the Second World War the *Seawolf* received thirteen battle stars and was presumed lost on 28 December 1944. (USN)

Launching party of the USS *Grenadier* (SS-*210*) at PNS. (USN)

The USS *Grenadier* was launched at PNS at 1130 hours on 25 November 1940. The steam tug *Sightseer* is standing by to guide the sub up to the dock. Before the war the *Sightseer* served as the ferry boat in the summertime to the Isles of Shoals. The *Grenadier* was commissioned on 1 May 1941 and was among the first line of attack submarine fleet in the Pacific War. She was sunk but the crew survived to spend two and a half years in Japanese prison camps. She received four battle stars.

Mrs S.S. Kennedy christening the USS *Sea Devil* (SS-400) at PNS on 28 February 1944. (PNSM)

Crew and officers of the *Sea Devil* with their families. The crew earned the *Sea Devil* five battle stars and rescued several downed aviators during the Second World War. They made a 'Down the throat' kill of a Japanese cargo ship. The sub was in the Yellow Sea when the war ended. (PNSM)

Ralph Styles, commander of the USS *Sea Devil*. (PNSM)

Crew of the *Sea Devil* possibly while in Pearl Harbor. Commander Styles is center front row with plaque. (PNSM)

USS *Trout* (SS-202) was built at PNS and commissioned on 15 November 1940. She evacuated 20 tons of gold from Corregidor. When shipment was off-loaded in Pearl Harbor one bar was missing. After a thorough search the missing ingot was found in the galley where the cook was using it as a paperweight. The sub received eleven battle stars during the Pacific War along with Presidential Unit Citations for 2nd, 3rd, and 5th war patrols. The *Trout* was lost in war, presumed sunk in the South China Sea while attacking a convoy, 17 April 1944. (USN)

Of the 20,000 workers employed at PNS during the Second World War many were women, who distinguished themselves at their various jobs including welding. (PNSM)

The USS *Balao* (SS-285) was built at PNS and commissioned on 4 February 1943. She conducted ten war patrols in the Pacific War and sunk over 32,000 tons of Japanese shipping. She received nine battle stars. (USN)

USS *Pollack* (SS-180), on the left, was commissioned at PNS on 15 January 1937. This sub sank the *Unkai Maru #1* on 7 January 1942, which marked the first confirmed kill for Pacific Fleet Submarine Force in the Second World War. During the war she conducted eleven war patrols and received ten battle stars. After the war she served as a training sub in New London, Conn. She was decommissioned on 21 September 1945. The other sub is the *Plunger*. (USN)

The presentation of the 1943 Safety Award for improvement to the sheet metal shop at PNS. (PNSM)

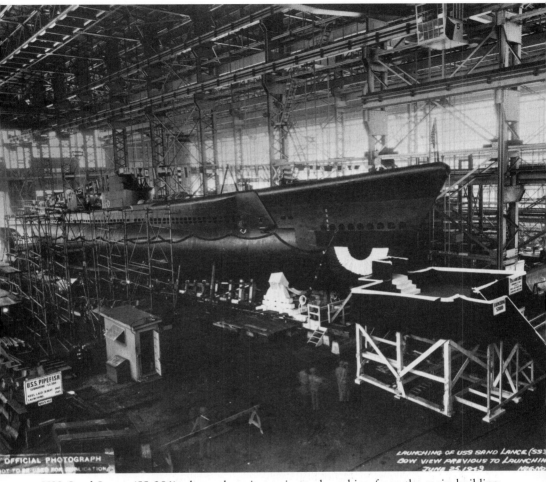

USS *Sand Lance* (SS-381), shown here just prior to launching from the main building ways at PNS. She was commissioned on 9 October 1943. After setting six torpedoes loose in a Japanese convoy (with all hitting their marks) the *Sand Lance* spent the next sixteen hours surviving a barrage of 100 depth charges! This first war patrol for the sub warranted a Presidential Unit Citation. The sub also received five battle stars. After the war the *Sand Lance* was used in the lend/lease program and sent to Brazil as part of a military assistance program. She was decommissioned in 1972. (PNSM)

The electronics office at PNS, *c.* 1940. (PNSM)

An unknown sub being launched at PNS. (PNSM)

The barracks and shops, which were built by prisoners, in front of the prison at PNS. (PNSM)

Workers at a blacksmith shop, showing a 12,000 lb forging hammer, *c.* 1940. (PNSM)

Presentation of forty-year service pins to Portsmouth Naval Shipyard employees on 16 February 1945. They were presented by RAdm. Thomas Withers, USN commandant. (PNSM)

USS *Sand Lance* steaming flank speed off Portsmouth Harbor. (USN)

Navy yard commandant Admiral Withers, USN, and shipyard civilians and military officers displaying Army/Navy 'E' Award on 17 March 1944. The three stars signify the third renewal of recognition for outstanding productivity during the Second World War. PNS was the most active construction yard on the east coast during the war. (PNSM)

On 17 August 1945 USS *Razorback* (SS-394), on the left of this photograph, joined eleven other US subs which sailed into Tokyo Harbor during the formal surrender of Japan. During the war she received five battle stars, as well as four stars during the Vietnam War. She was converted after the war in the GUPPY conversion program, and was sold to Turkey on 30 November 1970.

USS *Redfish* (SS-395), in the center, sank 42,000 tons of Japanese shipping, and received two battle stars. *Redfish* was used in Walt Disney's *20,000 Leagues Under the Sea* in 1954. She was also used in the 1957 film *Run Silent, Run Deep*. She was eventually sunk as a bombing target after decommissioning on 27 June 1968.

USS *Ronquil* (SS-397) is on the right. During her fourth war patrol the *Ronquil* rescued ten US aviators from a downed B-29. She also received six battle stars. After the war she was streamlined and equipped with a new propulsion system in the GUPPY conversion program. (USN)

Launching day for the *Razorback*, *Redfish* and *Ronquil*, 27 January 1944. (PNSM)

The steam locomotive #L-4 was still in use at PNS during and after the Second World War. This photograph was taken in 1947. (PNSM)

Shortly after the end of the Second World War approximately twelve German U-boats were brought to PNS for yard engineers to study their advance technologies. (PNSM)

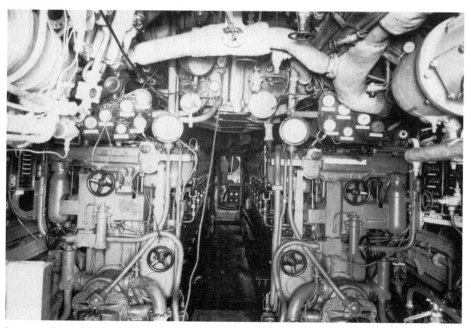

Interior shot of the engine room of the U-873, looking aft on 24 July 1946. (PNSM)

German U-boat, U-*3008*, shown here off PNS with a US crew on board after the Second World War, was built at Bremen, Germany, 1944–5. She surrendered to the Allies in Kiel, Germany, in May 1945. She was overhauled at PNS and put into service for the US Navy on 24 July 1946 and sold for scrap in 1955. (PNSM)

U-873, dubbed the 'sea cow,' in PNS dry dock. (PNSM)

A captured U-boat crew at PNS in 1945. Many POWs were sent to the yard prison until repatriated. (PNSM)

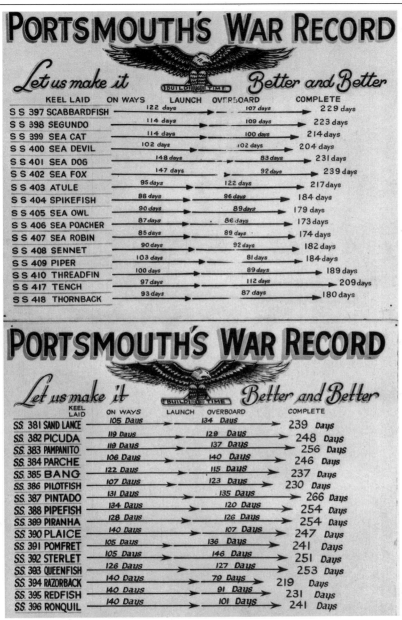

PORTSMOUTH'S WAR RECORD

Let us make it   Better and Better

	KEEL LAID	ON WAYS	LAUNCH	OVERBOARD	COMPLETE
S S 397 SCABBARDFISH		122 days		107 days	229 days
S S 398 SEGUNDO		114 days		109 days	223 days
S S 399 SEA CAT		114 days		100 days	214 days
S S 400 SEA DEVIL		102 days		102 days	204 days
S S 401 SEA DOG		148 days		83 days	231 days
S S 402 SEA FOX		147 days		92 days	239 days
S S 403 ATULE		95 days		122 days	217 days
S S 404 SPIKEFISH		88 days		96 days	184 days
S S 405 SEA OWL		90 days		89 days	179 days
S S 406 SEA POACHER		87 days		86 days	173 days
S S 407 SEA ROBIN		85 days		89 days	174 days
S S 408 SENNET		90 days		92 days	182 days
S S 409 PIPER		103 days		81 days	184 days
S S 410 THREADFIN		100 days		89 days	189 days
S S 417 TENCH		97 days		112 days	209 days
S S 418 THORNBACK		93 days		87 days	180 days

PORTSMOUTH'S WAR RECORD

Let us make it   Better and Better

	KEEL LAID	ON WAYS	LAUNCH	OVERBOARD	COMPLETE
S.S. 381 SAND LANCE		105 Days		134 Days	239 Days
S.S. 382 PICUDA		119 Days		129 Days	248 Days
S.S. 383 PAMPANITO		119 Days		137 Days	256 Days
S.S. 384 PARCHE		106 Days		140 Days	246 Days
S.S. 385 BANG		122 Days		115 Days	237 Days
S.S. 386 PILOTFISH		107 Days		123 Days	230 Days
S.S. 387 PINTADO		131 Days		135 Days	266 Days
S.S. 388 PIPEFISH		134 Days		120 Days	254 Days
S.S. 389 PIRANHA		128 Days		126 Days	254 Days
S.S. 390 PLAICE		140 Days		107 Days	247 Days
S.S. 391 POMFRET		105 Days		136 Days	241 Days
S.S. 392 STERLET		105 Days		146 Days	251 Days
S.S. 393 QUEENFISH		126 Days		127 Days	253 Days
S.S. 394 RAZORBACK		140 Days		79 Days	219 Days
S.S. 395 REDFISH		140 Days		91 Days	231 Days
S.S. 396 RONQUIL		140 Days		101 Days	241 Days

Samples of the impressive submarine construction war record of PNS, unequalled by any other shipyard on the east coast. The efforts of the thousands of shipyard workers had a tremendous impact on the naval warfront, especially in the Pacific Ocean, where PNS subs played a big role defeating the Japanese Navy. PNS workers continued their leadership role into the post-war era. (PNSM)

USS *Scorpion* (SS-278) was commissioned on 1 October 1942 and was lost during the war after approximately four war patrols and receiving three battle stars. The *Scorpion* was declared lost on 6 March 1944. This photo of the sub as she sits in Portsmouth Harbor, with the Naval Prison and shipyard in the background, pays tribute to all of the submarines and crew lost during the Second World War, who are considered 'Still on Patrol'. (PNSM)

Modern Submarine Era

Aerial view of PNS in 1954. (PNSM)

The SS-282. Post-Second World War was a transitional period for the submarine fleet before the nuclear age. Veteran war subs were converted into a sleeker and faster class fleet sub: the GUPPYs – G-reater U-nderwater P-ropulsion P-ower – the Y being added to make it phonetically more appealing. (PNSM)

The USS *Bonita* (SS-K-3), one of twenty subs which was converted in the GUPPY program at PNS. (USN)

An unidentified sub converted in the GUPPY program. (PNSM)

WAVE RECRUITING DRIVE
New England Company

Official Statement by the
Governors of:

CONNECTICUT	**NEW HAMPSHIRE**
MAINE	**RHODE ISLAND**
MASSACHUSETTS	**VERMONT**

We, the Governors of the New England States, urge all State and Local Government officials as well as the general public, to support actively the formation of the first "New England WAVE Company" and thus justify the trust which the United States Navy has placed in New England for choosing it as the first regional area to initiate the organization of a special company of WAVES during peacetime.

The WAVES of the United States Navy have served diligently and faithfully in accepting the highest responsibility in the service of their country, both in time of war and peace.

We urge the young women of New England to consider this splendid opportunity to contribute to the outstanding record which has earned Navy Women an honored and respected position on our defense team.

Signed:

Governor of Connecticut	*Governor of Maine*	*Governor of Massachusetts*

Recruiting declaration, *c.* 1955, for a 'New England Wave Company', signed by six NE governors: Ribicoff, Conn; Muskie, ME; Herter, MA; Divinell, NH; Roberts, RI; and Johnson, VT. (NHC)

The USS *Albacore* (SS-569). The research and development at PNS involved in designing a new submersible hull, which would allow new generations to conduct patrols for an unlimited time far below the surface, resulted in the launching of the *Albacore*, which was commissioned on 5 December 1953. All modern fast attack nuclear subs are direct descendants of the *Albacore*. She was decommissioned on 1 September 1972. (USN)

The *Albacore* is secured alongside the quay at PNS. The revolutionary hull design and propulsion system allowed *Albacore* to set numerous underwater speed records which are still classified. Mooring bollards serve as a reminder of the US Navy's heritage, they were once cannons of nineteenth century or earlier vintage. Today *Albacore* is located on Market Street, Portsmouth, NH, where she is open to the public. (USN)

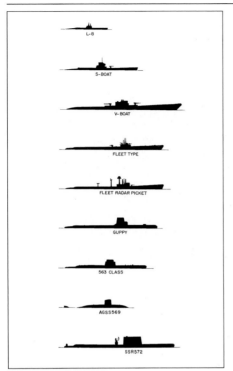

The evolution of the twentieth-century submarine fleet, 1917 to 1950s. (PNSM)

The transitional period for submarines from the end of the Second World War to 1953 with the building of the *Albacore* (SS-569). (PNSM)

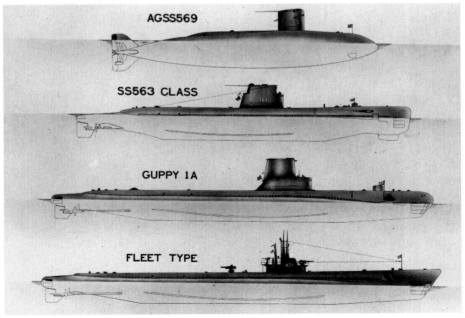

Memorial Day Parade, Market Square, Portsmouth, c. 1960. (PNSM)

Admiral Palmer, PNS commander, in conference with department heads. (PNSM)

Hull assembly at PNS. Bars of steel are being bent for use as submarine frames. The structural high yield steel can withstand water pressure several hundred feet below the surface. (PNSM)

PNS foundry. (PNS)

This photograph shows the end section of a submarine pressure hull being prepared for welding. The framing of a tapered hull section is in the background. (PNSM)

Translation of submarine plans from blueprint to steel began in the mold loft of the shipfitter's shop, as seen here. Photo by B. Gallagher, NYC. (USN)

The USS *Thresher* (SS-593), commissioned on 3 August 1961, is on its way down to the Piscataqua River on launching day. The PNS workers were particularly proud of this sub as she marked their contribution in designing a whole new class sub, the *593s* or *Thresher*-Class. Tragically the *Thresher* was lost with all hands on a test dive 200 miles east of Cape Code on 9 April 1963. (USN)

PNS foundry. (PNSM)

PNS foundry. (PNSM)

The USS *Dolphin* (SS-555), the 'Nichol Boat', was commissioned on 17 August 1968. She was the first non-nuclear sub built at PNS in ten years and served as a deep-dive research vessel. The photograph shows her being launched. (USN)

Machine shop at the shipyard in the 1960s. (PNSM)

Welding aboard a sub. (PNSM)

PNS workers with plans and blueprints for submarines. (PNSM)

USS *Grayling* (SSN-646) was launched at PNS on 22 June 1967 and was designed to serve as a fast attack sub. As seen underway off the coast of Portsmouth on 12 September 1969. (USN)

Workers installing torpedo tubes in the 1960s. Tubes were designed, manufactured and tested at PNS. (USN)

The USS *Sand Lance* (SSN-660) was launched on 11 November 1969 at PNS and marked the last sub built there, number 134, since 1917. She was a fast attack nuclear sub designed to run silent and deep. The *Sand Lance* was commissioned on 25 September 1971 and was 292 ft long, with a speed of more than 20 kn and a dive depth of over 400 ft. Her crew was made up of twelve officers and ninety-five enlisted men. She was equipped with four torpedo tubes. After twenty years of service the *Sand Lance* returned to PNS for overhaul. (USN)

The USS *Nathanael Greene* (SSBN-636) on the day of her official keel laying, 21 May 1962. Being the 131st submarine built at PNS, the *Greene* was one of just three Ballistic Missile subs built at Portsmouth. (USN)

The USS *Nathanael Greene*, the heaviest and largest sub ever constructed at PNS, was launched bow first from building ways at PNS on 12 May 1964. She was the last of the Ballistic Missiles to be built at PNS and was named after the famous revolutionary war general from Rhode Island. (PNSM)

The USS *John Adams* (*SSBN-620*) during commissioning ceremonies at PNS on 12 May 1964. She was designed as a Polaris Missile launching sub and was the seventeenth of her class built for the navy. She served sixteen North Atlantic patrols before being transferred to the Pacific where she conducted sixteen more patrols. The *John Adams* was converted to *Poseidon* Class at PNS. These subs manufactured their own oxygen which allowed them to remain 'down' for weeks on end.

Roland Phillips, shop 64 joiner, while working in Building #18 on mock-ups for AGSS-569 (*Albacore*), SSN-593 (*Thresher*), and their engine rooms. (USN)

The *Thresher* memorial service at the Mall, PNS, on 15 April 1963. Note the *Squalus* memorial to the right and the end of Building #86 where the Treaty of Portsmouth was signed. Quarters 'A' is in the left background behind the Polaris Missile. (PNSM)

United States Navy seaman raising the Stars and Stripes aboard his sub, *c.* 1976. (PNSM)

In and Around the Yard

Portsmouth Navy Yard Prison, the Disciplinary Command which once held over 3,000 military prisoners during the Second World War, was closed in 1974. (PNSM)

A military display in front of the Marine Barracks during the Bicentennial celebrations on 5 July 1976. (PNSM)

The bell from the battleship *New Hampshire* (BB-25), which sits in the Mall at PNS, as seen in 1976. The *New Hampshire* was commissioned on 19 March 1908 at New York Shipbuilding Corp., and served as a flagship for naval forces in Haitian waters 1920–1. (PNSM)

Buildings 60 and 59 viewed from Gate #1 on the Kittery side in 1987. (USN)

Shop 72, Riggers, Building #7, in 1976. (USN)

Building #15, Safety Office/Post Office at PNS. (USN)

An unknown submarine under construction in 1938, possibly the *Squalus* or the *Sculpin*. (USN)

Woodworking shop. (USN)

The Officers' Club was built in the 1850s as an ordnance facility to manufacture gun carriages for vessels of war outfitted at PNS. (USN)

Aerial view of PNS Navy Regional Hospital. Built in 1914, it closed as a hospital in 1974 and has served as the yard medical clinic since. (PNSM)

Dedication of Fletcher Field, a ballpark. (PNS)

Dedication plaque honoring
Captain C. Douglass Fletcher.
(PNS)

The dining-room of Quarters 'A', the home of the yard's commandant and family. (USN)

The living-room of Quarters 'A' is identical to the dining-room and even shares a duel fireplace. The Quarters 'A' booklet declares that 'Mouldings, decor, and basic construction are indicative of the requirements of a ship's master of a sleek clipper ship . . . she's as "clean as a boatswain's whistle".' (USN)

Stable/garage of Quarters 'A'. (USN)

The family dining area in Quarters 'A' was once a central part of life in this house and served as the main cooking and heating area as it was equipped with a massive fireplace. A hand-dug well could be accessed through the door shown in the photograph. (USN)

Shipyard built navy boat off Portsmouth Harbor, with Wentworth-by-the-Sea in the left background.

US Naval Reserve Training Center stopped serving in this capacity in 1980s. It was built during WWII. (USN)

Mine sweeper USS *Grouse*, secured in front of the Reserve Center, was used for Naval Reserve training. (PNSM)

Building #14. (USN)

Officers' Quarters 'O' was built around 1910. (PNSM)

Hard hat diver along the waterfront at PNS. (PNSM)

The Thresher Memorial Chapel, as seen in 1971, was built during the Second World War on the shipyard. (USN)

Interior of chapel. (USN)

'Review' during the launching ceremonies of USS *Seadragon* (SSN-*584*) in August 1958. (USN)

US Marine Corps mascot. (USN)

Quarters 'B' and 'C/D' were among the old classic houses of the yard, with 'B' completed in 1849. Foundations for 'C/D' were begun in 1828 and it was finished in 1834. They were established as officers' quarters and were built over an area known for its wild strawberry beds. (PNSM)

Quarters 'C/D' were built in the early part of the nineteenth century as officers' quarters. (PNSM)

View of the quarters on the yard, with the industrial section in the background. This was the residence of the commanding officer of PNS Prison. (USN)

Relief Drive function of SEA. (PNSM)

Portsmouth Naval Shipyard Cemetery, with graves dating back to 1821. (USN)

United States Marine Corps group photo taken in front of their barracks. (PNSM)

Gate #2 access to PNS from Kittery. (USN)

Portsmouth Naval Shipyard Museum volunteer Joseph Frost, shown here treating rare books. (PNSM)

Volunteer David Felton working in the ship's model shop at the PNS Museum. (PNSM)

PNS Museum curator Jim Dolph is on the left, standing with Commander Ralph Styles and a model of the commander's submarine which he served on in the Second World War, the *Sea Devil* (SS-400), 1990. (PNSM)

Visitors to PNS viewing items on display. (PNSM)

Visitors viewing the piece of flooring where Komura stood during the signing ceremonies of the Treaty of Portsmouth on 5 September 1905, on display today in Building #86. (PNSM)

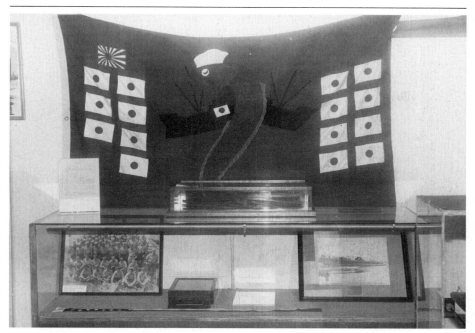

USS *Sand Lance* memorabilia. (PNSM)

Model of USS *Ranger* as seen in the 1930s. She was built for a parade in the town of Kittery. (PNSM)

Watch tower for the marine guard at the Naval Disciplinary Command, PNS, 5 April 1964. (PNSM)

The USS *Dallas* (SSN-700) as she looked entering Portsmouth Harbor to undergo an overhaul at PNS. Filming of Tom Clancy's *Hunt For Red October* went on without her, and a stand-in sub had to be used. (USN)

Gate #1, day's end. (PNSM)